GIANTS IN ACTION. *All Weights Wrestling Final at Grasmere 1971. Wilf Brocklebank (right) comes to grips with Peter Hunter (left). Brocklebank (nineteen stone) won by two clear falls.*

GRASMERE'S GIANTS OF TODAY

© Rex Woods 1975
ISBN   0 904558 05 3

Printed in England by Calabre Printing Limited, Liss, Hampshire

GRASMERE'S GIANTS OF TODAY

REX WOODS

With line drawings by Gwenllian Woods
and photographs by the author

PUBLISHED BY THE SPUR PUBLICATIONS COMPANY
Hill Brow, Liss, Hampshire

PREFACE

My motive in compiling this pictorial record of recent achievements is to add somewhat to the surprisingly scanty amount of illustrated literature on the Grasmere Sports, and to place on record for posterity some of the names of Grasmere's Giants of Today. In so doing I hope to convey my own great pleasure derived from attending Grasmere Sports — a pleasure which increases with continuity and which I can thoroughly recommend to others who can be in or around the Lake District on the Thursday nearest to August 20th.

Seaton, Devon.   Rex Woods

ACKNOWLEDGEMENTS

To all the people who have provided me with information and encouragement in compiling this book I gratefully acknowledge their assistance so readily given. The universal approval which the preparation of this book seems to have evoked has made the task all the more enjoyable. Notably my thanks are due to:

G. A. Ashton, secretary of the Grasmere Sports Committee and organiser of the Sports, and his assistant, Miss P. B. Huddlestone, who as well as providing information and approval, also granted facilities for obtaining action photographs from the centre of the arena.

Ken Bunting, organiser of the trails at Grasmere, for accurate details of the Hound and Puppy Trails, and Victor Brownlee, trainer of Shannon, Grasmere's most famous hound in recent years, for information on hound-training.

Fred Reeves and Tommy Sedgwick, fell-racing Giants of To-day, for describing their feelings before, during and after their famous victories in the Guides' Race.

A. E. Dennison, a leading wrestling umpire and for many years treasurer of the Association Governing Cumberland and Westmorland Style of Wrestling, for much information and various rule-books; and all the wrestling fraternity, who, apart from providing the subject-matter for many of the photographs, have without exception proved most forthcoming and enthusiastic over the idea of this book. If there exists a discourteous or unsporting Cumberland and Westmorland wrestler, I have not met him.

Finally, and by no means least, I want to express my grateful thanks to my wife for her drawings of local scenes, which help convey the atmosphere of the Grasmere setting, which forms the background against which these stirring Lakeland events take place.

R. W.

CONTENTS

Chapter		Page
1	THE LAKELAND SETTING	8
2	THE GUIDES' RACES	19
	THE WINNERS FROM 1868	34
3	THE HOUND TRAILS	37
4	CUMBERLAND AND WESTMORLAND WRESTLING	51
	GRASMERE'S WRESTLING CHAMPIONS FROM 1852	61
	ACTION PICTURES	65
5	THE WRESTLING RULES	79
	GLOSSARY OF WRESTLING TERMS	85
	COMPETITORS IN 1974 - ALL WEIGHTS	89
	MEMBERS AND OFFICIALS OF GRASMERE SPORTS, 1974	91

PHOTOGRAPHS

Frontispiece : All Weights Final, 1971 - W. Brocklebank v P. Hunter

Page

15   The Setting for the Grasmere Sports

16   *(opposite, in colour)* Wrestling Costumes

23   Victory - Fred Reeves

26   Son emulates father - Christopher Hartley

29   The Record - Fred Reeves

32   Moment of fulfilment - Tom Sedgwick

42   The Start - Hounds rush past the trailer

43   First obstacle. Hound Trail at Grasmere, 1974

44   Anticipation

45   Refreshment

48   Shannon

48   *(opposite, in colour)* The Hound Trail and Guides' Race starts

54   Stone wall builder versus shepherd - W. Brocklebank v P. Hunter

PHOTOGRAPHS (continued)

55   Taking hold - John Dennison v Tom Harrington

59   Family Record - Joe, Jim and Tom Harrington

65   *(opposite, in colour)* Spectacular fall - G. Younger v I. Armstrong

67   Who's fall? - P. Hayhurst v W. Brocklebank, Junior

68   Both Hold, Going! Going! Gone! W. Brocklebank v D. Dayson

70   World Champion - T. Harrington v J. Dennison

71   Landing with a thud - J. Dennison v H. Brocklebank

72   Battle of the Giants - W. Brocklebank v J. Barnes

73   Historic moment at Grasmere - W. Bland v S. Dalton

74   Brotherly encounter - H. Brocklebank v W. Brocklebank, Junior

75   Moment of sensation - A. Davidson v W. Brocklebank

76   Shepherd versus schoolmaster - P. Hunter v R. Robson

77   Hunter's fall - P. Hunter v R. Robson

THE OLD BRIDGE HOUSE,
AMBLESIDE

THE LAKELAND SETTING

The Lakeland Setting

THE BACKGROUND

For those fortunate enough to live within reach, the summer season of Lakeland sports meetings provides competitors and spectators alike with a succession of enjoyable outings in breathtaking settings. For those who live at a greater distance, the name that conjures up the greatest excitement and tradition is that of the famous Grasmere sports, usually held on the Thursday nearest to August 20th.

The appeal to the outsider lies partly in the splendour of the setting, beside Lake Grasmere, with glorious views of the surrounding fells in whichever direction one looks; partly, too, in the atmosphere and tradition that pervades the arena — with the Earl of Lonsdale, like his forbears, officiating in the centre. But for anyone new to Lakeland sports, perhaps the greatest appeal lies in the three sports which characterise them:

1. Guides' Races.
2. Hound Trails.
3. Cumberland and Westmorland style Wrestling.

All are to be seen at their keenest and best at Grasmere. Other more familiar track and field events play an integral part in the day's enjoyment, but for the visitor the novelty lies in the three widely divergent, but equally intriguing, contests mentioned. It is on these that I propose to dwell.

Chapter 1

In all three it would be rewarding to delve into the past, but it is on the Giants of Today that I propose to focus. For it is these men who are maintaining a great local tradition, and are surely worthy of our attention. Without them — fell-racers, athletes, wrestlers, as well as the durable hounds which race over, the fells — our heritage would be the poorer. It is largely this tradition which induces the fell-racers to train and compete up and down the fells, and the wrestlers to wrestle, and owners of hounds to race them far and wide. It is true that the runners and wrestlers compete for prize-money, and are thus professionals, and that a sizeable volume of betting takes place in hound-trailing. But they are only part-time professionals, some of whom can be successful enough to supplement their incomes earned at their various jobs. It is the enjoyment of competition and achievement, of making and meeting friends throughout the district, rather than the monetary reward alone, which attracts the competitors.

Of course counter-attractions and diversions of the modern age tend to lure away a proportion of potential competitors. But, conversely, modern transport and modern wages make it easier for some to reach the Lakeland sports meetings throughout the summer. A race up the fell in the Guides' Race is no longer preceded by a ten or twenty mile walk over the fells to get there, as was the case in the early days.

Yearning for bygone days is a fruitless pastime. But being aware of, and grateful for, the perpetuation of a long-standing tradition can be far more beneficial, and the performers of today deserve our gratitude and appreciation.

LANDMARKS IN HISTORY

There is some difficulty in recording all changes and events which have taken place. However, it is worthwhile noting a number of important dates which are as follows:

1852   The origin of Grasmere Sports is lost in antiquity, but in this year they are known to have been held, in April, in Hudson's field, adjoining the Red Lion.

1870   The venue was moved to Pavement End, and the date to August, with summer visitors in mind.

1904   The Sports were moved to Broadgate Meadow, New Field, adjoining Grasmere Hall, where they continued to be held until World War I, during which they were suspended.

1919   On resumption after the war, the sports were held in the present field, which gives a superb view of the Guides' Race up to Butter Crag, and the Hound Trail which winds across the surrounding fells and saddles; the site also provides easy access to the public.

From early days the Grasmere Sports included Wrestling, a Guides' Race, and a Hound Trail and these three characteristic events continue in their traditional form today.

Change for the sake of change is clearly not the policy of Grasmere. Rather, the aim is the perpetuation of a worthwhile tradition. To implement this policy, the Grasmere Sports Committee was registered as a limited liability company in 1925. The committee and the long-serving secretary, G. A. Ashton, and his able assistant, Miss P. B. Huddlestone, deserve our gratitude for their work towards this end. Lakeland sports are surely a worthy part of our national heritage.

A section of an early programme of the Sports is given opposite. This refers to the events for August 20th, 1936.

THE WORLD-FAMED OLD ENGLISH GAMES
under Royal Patronage

GRASMERE AND LAKELAND DISTRICT ANNUAL

ATHLETIC SPORTS
(The Grasmere Sports Committee Ltd.)

PROGRAMME & LIST OF ENTRIES
THURSDAY, AUGUST 20th, 1936.

The Sports commence at 12-0 noon with the Light Weights (9st. 7lbs). Wrestling, to be succeeded by Heavy Weight Wrestling (for the Association Championship Challenge Cup), Middle Weights (11st.) all in costume.

12 noon —Long Leap.	1-30 p.m.—Adults' Pole Leap.	2-45 p.m.—Juveniles' Pole Leap.
12-15 p.m.—High Leap.	1-30 p.m.—Hound Trail.	
12-30 p.m.—Half-Mile Handicap.	2-0 p.m. —Pillow Fight.	3-0 p.m. —Guides' Race.
1-0 p.m. —Juvenile Guides' Race.	2-30 p.m.—Mile Handicap.	3-30 p.m.—Puppy Trail.

The Leaping Competitions will take place during the Wrestling.

Extra Prizes given for Special Feats.

Any of the Prizes may be increased or decreased at the will of the Committee.

Motor Char-a-bancs not allowed within 20 feet of the Ring Edge.

First-Class Refreshments opposite Grandstand by STORMS FARM DAIRY Ltd., Keswick.

PROGRAMME OF MUSIC BY THE

SEATON SILVER BAND
Musical Director - Mr. ALLAN HIGH

No.		Title	Composer
1.	March	" 3 D.G's "	Brophy
2.	Fox-trot	" When you're in Love "	—
3.	Cornet Solo	" Silver Threads "	—
4.	Fantasia	" Country Life "	Le Duc
5.	Selection	" Pirates of Penzance "	Sullivan
6.	March	" The Defender "	—
7.	Concert Waltz	" The Blue Danube "	Strauss
8.	Descriptive Piece	" Mississippi "	Rimmer
9.	Selection	" Desert Song "	Romberg
10.	Waltz	" Merry Widow "	Lehar
11.	Overture	" Overturania "	Bartram
12.	March	" The White Star "	—
13.	Fox-trot	" Lovely to look at "	—
14.	Novelty	" Three Blind Mice "	Williams
15.	Musical Comedy	" Student Prince "	Romberg
16.	Fantasia (Grasmere Speciality)	" John Peel "	Greenwood
17.	Overture	" Golconda "	Greenwood
18.	Selection	" Famous Songs "	D. Wright
19.	Waltzes	" Morning Glory "	Greenwood
20.	Fox-trot	" We saw the Sea "	—

GOD SAVE THE KING.

PRICE SIXPENCE

Printed with permission of The Grasmere Sports Committee Ltd.

The setting
for the Grasmere Sports

15

GEOGRAPHICAL NOTE

Much of the attraction of the Grasmere Sports lies in the charm of its setting. The village itself is built almost entirely of Lakeland stone, on level ground, with Lake Grasmere and its pleasant island in the middle, to the South. On the other three sides rise sheltering fells, high but not oppressive.

The village has the advantage of being by-passed, to the East, by the main Windermere-Keswick road, which means that though remaining accessible, Grasmere is not choked by traffic.

Grasmere has long been a centre from which to explore the Lake District, with a wide choice of walks and climbs within easy range. To the East, as a result of geographical faults dating from the ice-age, lies a series of long steep ridges, running from North to South. It is up the first of these that the Guides' Races are run, and which hounds traverse before rushing headlong down to the finish in the arena. A line due East would reach the Kirkstone Pass Inn, at a distance of four miles as the crow flies — but certainly more than that as the hiker hikes.

To the South-East, via the road which skirts the Northern side of Rydal Water, one reaches Ambleside, four miles away, at the Northern end of Lake Windermere. The town of Windermere itself is nine miles South-East of Grasmere.

South-West, at a similar distance, lies Lake Coniston. To the West, reached by a steep road over Red Bank, through the village of Chapel Stile, runs the Langdale Valley with the Langdale Pikes overlooking.

To the North and slightly West, lies Easedale, leading to an attractive waterfall descending from Easedale Tarn, which is up among the fells. Due North is the main road up to Keswick, thirteen miles away, passing Helvellyn (3,113 feet) to the East and Thirlmere, long and narrow, to the West.

Grasmere was known in Anglo-Saxon times as Grismer, a name of Viking origin meaning "Lake of the Wild Boar". Described by the poet William Wordsworth as "the loveliest spot that man hath ever known", Grasmere is still associated with his name. For Wordsworth's Dove Cottage, which he occupied with his sister, Dorothy, from 1799 to 1808, is within a stone's throw of the present sports field. Wordsworth later

WRESTLING COSTUMES, *with embroidery fore and aft.*
Left to right : Roger Dixon (Grasmere), Ivor Armstrong (Carlisle) and
Roger Wilkinson (Staveley) - in order of costume merit.

moved to Allan Bank on the West side of the lake, and finally to Rydal Mount, overlooking Rydal Water nearby. His grave is at St. Oswald's Church, right in the village of Grasmere, with the river Rothay flowing by.

Despite the crowds of visitors that such a charming village inevitably attracts, Grasmere retains its character, and the annual holding of the Grasmere Sports helps it to do so.

ASHNESS BRIDGE, Nʳ KESWICK

THE GUIDES' RACES

The Guides' Races

ATTRIBUTES OF A FELL-RACER

Fell-racing is essentially for the wiry, the dogged and the competitive. At Grasmere the Guides' Race is from the arena to a point on Butter Crag, rising steeply to the East, to a height of 966 feet (294 metres) and back. The Juvenile Guides' Race (under seventeen years of age) is round a cairn at 685 feet (209 metres).

Anyone who has walked the course can begin to appreciate the demands on the legs, lungs and courage of those who race to the top and then plunge downwards on rubbery legs, over uncertain ground. Some are footsure — others fall, to rise again. All compel admiration for their arduous exertion.

The physical attributes of a fell-racer obviously include a strong heart for the climb, and very sound ankles and knees for the descent. Most of the great champions have been men between the nine stone and ten stone marks, and of moderate height.

Chapter 2

The greatest of them all, W. Teasdale, M.B.E., of Caldbeck, was one of the smallest, at nine stone and five feet three inches. At the other end of the scale was Tom Conchie, a granite-breaker from Shap, who was six feet two inches, and weighed fourteen stone — an awesome weight to carry to the summit, but a valuable source of momentum for the descent, provided one's legs are strong enough. His carried him to five Grasmere victories.

The climb is done first at the run, then at a steady jog, and, in steep places, at a walk up to the first cairn on Butter Crag, and thence across rough ground to the further cairn whence the descent is made. Thus those descending headlong, avoid those who are still climbing to the first flag. Fell-racers develop their own style of descending, and have to weigh the risks of bold stag-like leaps which can win races, against possible disaster from untimely falls. When Bill Teasdale set up his record in 1965 (at the age of forty, incidentally), his time to the top was nine minutes forty seconds, and he raced down in three minutes twenty-five seconds, for a total of thirteen minutes five seconds.

Victory

FRED REEVES *after his third successive victory in 1971. Butter Crag, at a height of 965 feet, is in the background on the skyline. Reeves won at Grasmere at the first attempt, having previously reached fame as a runner on the flat. In 1969 he won the professional British Two Mile Track Championship, before concentrating on fell running.*

TRAINING

Training tends to vary with each competitor, according to physique and occupation. For instance Bill Teasdale's work on the farm, which took him many miles a day over the fells, as well as his regular fell-racing (he won thirteen times at Croglin, ten times in succession at Keswick, eight at Alva, and six each at Ambleside and Kilnsey), coupled with the lightness of his frame, rendered much further training superfluous. Fred Reeves, on the other hand, who works as an administrative assistant at Coniston Green Slate Company, runs consistently sixty to seventy miles a week when in training in the winter, and thirty to forty in the summer during the fell-racing season. Fell-racers are often trained in groups by former champions, particularly in the early stages, which makes this strenuous pastime less lonely. Tommy Sedgwick restarts his training in the New Year, working up to sixty to seventy miles a week of fell, cross-country and track running, by the start of the season, in May. The season ends in October, but Grasmere, in late August, is regarded as the climax.

At one time the race was open to both amateurs and professionals, but when the *Amateur Athletics Association* was formed in 1880, amateurs could no longer compete. Like the Wrestlers at Grasmere and at other Lakeland sports meetings, the fell-racers are professionals in that they compete for any prize-money that their considerable exertions may bring. But this is not to say that they make anything approaching a living at their sport. They are teachers, shepherds, quarrymen and office workers first, and race or wrestle primarily for pleasure, with the chance of some well-earned reward, making many friends in the process.

CHAMPION RUNNERS

Great names of the past include, in chronological order, with their respective number of victories in brackets: John Greenop, of Langdale (6); Tom Conchie, of Shap (5); Ernest Dalzell, a gamekeeper from Keswick (7), who might well have added to his total but for the First World War in which he lost his life — he was still winning in 1913; R. Robinson (6) and R. Gilpin (5), down to W. Teasdale (11), whose 1965 record no longer stands, as we shall see as we now focus on the engaging tussle of today's giants, Fred Reeves, of Coniston and Tommy Sedgwick, of New Hutton, near Kendal.

Fred Reeves, who is a former professional two-mile champion on the flat, is also an accomplished fell-racer. His strength lies in his speed up the fell, where his long, strong legs and light frame are his advantage. Tommy Sedgwick on the other hand, excels at hurtling down the fell. And herein has lain the excitement for those who have watched their struggles over recent years.

Reeves started with a victory at his first attempt in 1969, aged twenty-four, with Sedgwick, aged nineteen, runner-up. The same result followed in 1970 and 1971. But the bare results do not convey the full story.

In 1970, in pouring rain, with a helicopter (filming for television) hovering close above them as they climbed, Reeves turned at the flag with a lead of a hundred yards. On the descent, however, Sedgwick showed his mettle, plunging down the slippery slope. Despite falling three times, he had reduced Reeves' lead to thirty yards by the fell wall. Nearing the bottom of Hollens Breast he had overhauled Reeves, and taken a lead of a few yards. But by now his legs were rubbery, and Reeves' courage was still undaunted. Once on the flat, he pulled away to a worthy victory from a worthy challenger. In 1971, the conditions were dry and hot, and again Reeves reached the top with a long lead, estimated at two hundred and thirty yards. Anyone who did not know of Sedgwick's downhill burst might have thought that the race was as good as won. Reeves, mindful, no doubt, of the previous year's struggle, made no mistake, and still had thirty yards to spare at the finish, in the fast time of thirteen minutes nineteen seconds.

1972 saw Sedgwick's triumph, for which he had striven so valiantly and often. This time Reeves' lead at the turn was only twenty yards, and immediately sensing his opportunity at last, Sedgwick swooped down to win by some two hundred yards, in thirteen minutes seven seconds, only two seconds outside Teasdale's record. Reeves had suffered a knee injury the previous week, but sportingly stated that he never felt it in the race, and that even if he had been at his best he did not think that he could have beaten Tommy Sedgwick that day, adding "After all, he has just run twelve seconds faster than I have ever done".

And so to 1973, with the two champions still in great contention, Reeves having gained eleven victories over Sedgwick, who had three victories over Reeves, so far that season. An

SON EMULATES FATHER. *Christopher Hartley equalling the record in the Juvenile Guides' Race, 1972, at Grasmere. His father, Tyson Hartley, won this event in1939. The record, 9 mins. 17 secs., was set by Stan Edmondson of Seathwaite, Borrowdale, in 1966. Hartley, of Seathwaite, Broughton-in-Furness, was also successful the previous year, despite two crashing falls after negotiating the final wall. When the challenge to the supremacy of Reeves and Sedgwick comes, Hartley could be the one to provide it.*

added interest was the first run at Grasmere as a senior for young Christopher Hartley, of Seathwaite, who had emulated the 1939 feat of his father, Tyson Hartley, by winning the Juvenile Guides' Race in 1971 and had repeated the victory in 1972, equalling the record (nine minutes twenty-five seconds).

The race between Sedgwick and Reeves followed an almost identical pattern to that of the previous year, with Sedgwick proving that his 1972 victory was no fluke, by again getting within two seconds of Teasdale's record. Hartley confirmed his promise by taking third place in a field of ten, in front of another young fell-racer having his first senior race at Grasmere, Stephen Carr of Kendal — a portent, perhaps, of great challenges to come.

BREAKING THE RECORD

In 1974 Bill Teasdale's record, so nearly equalled by Tom Sedgwick in the two previous years, was broken by nearly eight seconds. Fred Reeves broke it, in twelve minutes fifty-seven and a half seconds, running the course in some twenty seconds less than he had ever achieved in his previous five attempts. Sedgwick, though not timed officially, must have again been close to, or within, the existing record, running very true to his form of the two previous years.

The sensational time by Reeves was attributable to a vastly improved descent — possibly allied to a handsomely increased first prize of seventy-five pounds, as against the twenty pounds which he received for each of his three previous victories. Though he had, as ever, a useful lead at the turn, it was not, judging by previous years, unassailable. But, though Sedgwick went after him. Reeves this time matched mastery at climbing with skilful and dashing descent, to achieve at the age of twenty-nine a glorious landmark in the history of the Grasmere Guides' Race.

With Hartley injured at work and unable to run, Stephen Carr moved up into third place. One hopes that there will always be men and youths with the courage to pursue this testing challenge of the fells, so that the Grasmere Guides' Race will continue to capture the imagination of visitors and locals alike, and help to keep the Grasmere Sports unique.

The Record

FRED REEVES *at the moment of his greatest Grasmere triumph, at the age of twenty-nine, breasting the tape in 1974, seven and a half seconds inside Bill Teasdale's record, set up in 1965, at the age of forty. Butter Crag, to which Reeves has just raced, is on the sky-line.*

FRED REEVES

For a vivid description of the race, stage by stage, from the fell runner's point of view, I quote the thoughts on the subject committed to paper for me by Fred Reeves not long after his record-breaking run in 1974. I have not presumed to "improve" upon his description. The thoughts and words are his; the thanks are surely ours, for conveying to us the feelings which we must all have tried to imagine, and can now share. He writes:

The event really starts at about 2 p.m. when we go into the dressing-rooms to change. The nervous laughter and the quiet hellos seem to say that friendship is going to turn into rivalry within the hour.

Half an hour to go and we are now in the arena warming up. The pressure and tension is rising steadily. You pray for the gun to go so that you can get out of the arena away from the crowds.

Once into the fell the steepness of the first field hits you hard; but once over the wall the going gets a little easier. A quick look behind to see how things are going and then push hard for the next hundred yards, to the first tree.

The first bit of walking now, up through the bracken and over the one or two rock outcrops and on to the track across the back of the fell. This part — wide enough for a car, but steep enough for only a Land-Rover to climb — is perhaps where the race is won or lost. To gain on the leader or to lose the pack behind you can give a tremendous advantage.

The last fifty yards up the crag is virtually hands and knees stuff, with loose rock, bracken and steepness really dragging you to a state of mental and physical tiredness; but something keeps dragging you up to that first flag. There it is! What a relief! The same old chap says to go round the back of the rock, but the twenty or so people there don't seem to want you to; so you scramble where you can.

The hundred yards between the two flags are perhaps the roughest of the race. The hidden rocks and rough tufts of grass are real ankle twisters. Round the second flag, throwing out your arm to collect your string and washer, jump the four or five feet off the crag, and down through the first patch of bracken. Out of the bracken and on to the steepest part of the descent, which is a real head-spinner if you stand and look down, not that you have much time for that at the moment! You have to keep your eyes open down this part for a large, but partly hidden, rock, which is the only marker to the track through the bracken.

The next section is fairly awkward — quite steep, and "sidey-banks"; that is with one foot always lower down the fell than the other while you are going across the fell. Through the bog, down a short steep section, round a left-hand curve, over a short rock outcrop and the realisation that in fifteen to twenty seconds you will be out of the bracken, heading for the arena.

At this point this year I stole a quick glance back, and couldn't see Tommy, and immediately realised I was in with a great chance.

Jump the beck, through the last twenty yards of bracken and there's a fence. Over this and there is only one steep field between you and victory. All the way down I had a feeling Tommy was catching me, but, with over a hundred yards lead here, I knew it was mine. The only thing in my mind was victory.

You notice the crowd thirty or forty yards from the road. But who cares now? The last hundred yards across the arena this year I eased up. If I had known about the record, I'm confident I'd have knocked a further three or four seconds off it; but not to worry — its mine now, so I'm happy.

The next ten or fifteen minutes were fantastic. Everyone clamouring round — photographers, reporters, family and friends. I was almost in tears with delight, and for the first time in my life I allowed myself the luxury of a lap of honour — on reflection, the hardest and longest four hundred metres I have ever run!

It's all over now, so into the changing-room, a quick rub-down from my trainer, a lovely shower and perhaps thirty minutes of re-running the race over and over again with the lads. No malice, no hard feelings; just delights and dis-appointments, but still great friends.

FOOTNOTE: For a detailed year by year history of the Guides' Race there is a very commendable illustrated publication on this subject, compiled in 1973 by two contemporary fell-racers, Michael Miller of Burneside and Denis Bland of Kendal. It is entitled *See the Conquering Hero Comes*, to which refrain the winner is traditionally welcomed back into the arena.

MOMENT OF FULFILMENT *for Tom Sedgwick. Victory in the Grasmere Guides's Race in 1972 - after three successive years as runner-up. He won again in 1973. On both occasions he was within two seconds of W. Teasdale's record, 13 minutes 5 seconds.*

TOMMY SEDGWICK

Likewise Tommy Sedgwick has described his thoughts and feelings as he remembers them from 1972, the year of his greatest moment at Grasmere so far. Here again I do not propose to tamper with his words. They surely give a more vivid impression of the agonies and ecstasies of the fell-runner than any attempted paraphrase could posssibly portray. He comments as follows:

Arrived early, as usual. Watched the Juniors, and then retreated to the changing-rooms, to look miserable and feel terrible, like the rest of the lads in there. The atmosphere is terrific; you could cut it with a knife — guess it means so much to all of us to do well.

About half past two I go out on to the track, try to relax and loosen up, but it seems in vain. My legs feel dead, my nerves tight. I feel like doing anything but run. When they call you to the line, nerves reach a peak. The gun goes off and nerves go instantly, oblivious to everything but the race.

The pace is fast — too fast! Fred and Tony Daly go through to the front up the first two fields. I feel tight, with two lads tucked in close behind me — hope they blow up; hope I don't. Over the wall, on to the fell. Fred has dropped Tony; as we start to climb, Tony comes back to me, and Fred is getting no farther away. The two lads behind fade. I get past Tony where the Junior and Senior courses split.

As we reach the path to the top, Fred and I have got away from the rest of the field. We climb the path. I feel, rather than know, that the distance beween us is lessening. I realise I'm a lot nearer than ever before. I think I can just keep it going. As we get nearer the first flag, I feel really rough, but keep thinking I must hang on, and maybe — just maybe!

As I reach the first flag, and across to the second, it goes through my mind that, if I can stay on my feet, I can catch him. I pass him down the steep clear stretch. He doesn't come with me and I feel relieved. Three-quarters of the way down I realise that, if I can stay on my feet, I can win. But my legs feel shaky.

When I get back to the road and can see the tape, I feel good. Great! I am going to win at last!

I can't explain how I felt after the race — just a mixture of tiredness and excitement.

THE WINNERS

Winners of the Guides' Race at Grasmere from 1868, the year of the first fell race.

1868	G. Birkett, Wythburn	1891	J. H. Harris, Patterdale
1869	G. Birkett, Wythburn	1892	C. Armstrong, Rydal
1870	W. Greenop, Langdale	1893	J. Pepper, Langdale
1871	G. Birkett, Wythburn	1894	T. Conchie, Shap
1872	J. Dwyer, Kirby Ireleth	1895	T. Conchie, Shap
1873	J. Birkett, Wythburn	1896	T. Conchie, Shap
1874	J. Park, Ambleside	1897	T. Conchie, Shap
1875	J. Dwyer, Kirby Ireleth	1898	T. Taylor, Skelwith
1876	J. Greenop, Langdale	1899	T. Taylor, Skelwith
1877	J. Greenop, Langdale	1900	T. Conchie, Shap
1878	J. Greenop, Langdale	1901	J. C. Murray, Falstone
1879	J. Greenop, Langdale	1902	J. C. Murray, Falstone
1880	J. Greenop, Langdale	1903	J. C. Murray, Falstone
1881	J. Greenop, Langdale	1904	J. C. Murray, Falstone
1882	E. Collins, Dalton	1905	E. Dalzell, Keswick
1883	E. Collins, Dalton	1906	E. Dalzell, Keswick
1884	D. Mossop, Dalton	1907	E. Dalzell, Weswick
1885	R. Lancaster, Rusland	1908	E. Dalzell, Keswick
1886	R. Lancaster, Force Forge	1909	E. Dalzell, Keswick
1887	R. Lancaster, Force Forge	1910	E. Dalzell, Keswick
1888	J. Grizedale, Grasmere	1911	J. R. Fleming, Backbarrow
1889	R. Lancaster, Satterthwaite	1912	J. R. Fleming, Backbarrow
1890	J. Grizedale, Grasmere	1913	E. Dalzell, Keswick

Grasmere Sports were abandoned during the war. On the rersumption they were moved to the present field.

1919	J. Pooley, Hawkshead	1930	J. James, Hincaster
1920	G. Woolcock, Langdale	1931	J. McCabe, Distington
1921	G. Woolcock, Langdale	1932	R. Gilpin, Braithwaite
1922	G. Woolcock, Langdale	1933	R. Gilpin, Braithwaite
1923	R. Robinson, Newby Bridge	1934	R. Gilpin, Braithwaite
1924	R. Robinson, Newby Bridge	1935	J. W. Conkey, Lorton
1925	R. Robinson, Newby Bridge	1936	R. Gilpin, Braithwaite
1926	R. Robinson, Newby Bridge	1937	R. Gilpin, Braithwaite
1927	J. James, Oxenholme	1938	J. W. Conkey, Lorton
1928	R. Robinson, Newby Bridge	1939	R. Thwaites, Braithwaite
1929	R. Robinson, Newby Bridge		

The Sports were again abandoned for the duration of the Second World War.

1946 D. Temple, Ennerdale
1947 S. Edmondson, Borrowdale
1948 S. Edmondson, Borrowdale
1949 C. Brown, Troutbeck
1950 W. Teasdale, Caldbeck
1951 S. Edmonson, Borrowdale
1952 W. Teasdale, Caldbeck
1953 W. Teasdale, Caldbeck
1954 W. Teasdale, Caldbeck
1955 W. Teasdale, Caldbeck
1956 W. Teasdale, Caldbeck
1957 R. Harrison, Oxenpark
1958 W. Teasdale, Caldbeck
1959 R. Harrison, Stainton
1960 W. Teasdale, Caldbeck

1961 W. Teasdale, Caldbeck
1962 R. Harrison, Newton-in-Furness
1963 R. Morton, Wigton
1964 R. Morton, Wigton
1965 W. Teasdale, Caldbeck
1966 W. Teasdale, Caldbeck
1967 R. Harrison, Ulverston
1968 T. Garside, Hawkshead
1969 F. Reeves, Barrow
1970 F. Reeves, Barrow
1971 F. Reeves, Coniston
1972 T. Sedgwick, New Hutton
1973 T. Sedgwick, New Hutton
1974 F. Reeves, Coniston

Winners of the Juvenile Guides' Race, which was introduced in 1920.

1920 E. Edwards
1921 J. Hanratty
1922 B. McGhie
1923 E. Edwards
1924 J. Blenkharn
1925 J. Stables
1926 J. Lancaster
1927 D. Drinkall
1928 J. W. Gaskell
1929 T. Hutchinson
1930 W. Conkey
1931 A. Drinkall
1932 R. Thwaites
1933 D. Temple
1934 W. Hoggarth
1935 W. Hoggarth
1936 J. Smith

1937 H. Hardy
1938 J. Staveley
1939 T. Hartley

1946 T. W. Moore
1947 B. Palmer
1948 M. White
1949 R. Sill
1950 R. Sill
1951 R. Brockbank
1952 J. Gibson
1953 J. Gibson
1954 J. Hicks
1955 A. Denby
1956 N. Taylor
1957 D. Moss
1958 D. Moss

1959 D. Robinson
1960 M. Fiddler
1961 K. Shuttleworth
1962 G. Sibson
1963 F. Haddow
1964 J. Stretch
1965 T. Sedgwick
1966 S. Edmondson
1967 P. Proctor
1968 P. Proctor
1969 J. Carruthers
1970 R. Ellwood
1971 C. Hartley
1972 C. Hartley
1973 G. Moffat
1974 B. Robinson

THE HOUND TRAILS

The Hound Trails

THE RULES

The *Hound Trailing Association* was founded in 1906, and it publishes a book of regulations for the guidance of members and trail organisers. This book is constantly revised and kept up-to-date. As well as the central committee of the Association there are eight area committees, which supervise hound trailing in their own areas, which are as follows : Aspatria and Wigton; Carlisle; Cockermouth and Workington; Keswick; Penrith; Ulverston; Westmorland; Whitehaven.

The regulations stipulate that the season shall be from April 1st (or Easter Saturday, if earlier) until October 31st. It is also laid down that there shall be no trails on Sundays, nor any without the consent of the farmers over whose land the trail runs.

Chapter 3

The regulations also deal fully with the registration of hounds. The birth of a litter must be reported within three days. At six weeks registration is required, and a further six weeks later the ear-marking is carried out by an official of the association. As well as age and ear-number, pedigree and colour are recorded. As with racehorses, the age of a hound is taken from January 1st in the hound's year of birth. A puppy remains eligible to compete in Puppy Trails until the end of the year following its year of birth. Names, once they are registered, may not be changed during a season. Nor may the names of famous hounds be re-used. It is stated unequivocally that any hound that worries sheep shall be struck off the register.

LAYING THE TRAIL

There are also precise instructions for the laying of trails. There shall be not more than three trailers for each trail. There shall be a minimum of six scouts to guard the trail when laid. Ken Bunting, who has been trail organiser at Grasmere in recent years enlists the help of two perennial trailers, both shepherds,

J. Hardisty and T. Graves, who have performed this arduous task for some thirty years. In 1974 there were nineteen scouts for the hound trail and nine for the puppy trail, which would indicate that little is left to chance in this respect.

The trail mixture is prescribed as follows: two fluid ounces of aniseed; half an ounce of turpentine; seventy-four ounces of best paraffin oil. Heavy oil to be added when necessary.

Even the size of the trail rag is stated — not less than two feet in length and six inches in breadth, with not less than six feet of cord attached. All rags must be made of woollen material. Anyone who has ever caught the strong whiff of the trail rag as the trailer scales the last fell wall and drags it into the arena at Grasmere will agree that the prescribed mixture is a most potent and effective brew!

THE TRAIL ROUTES

At Grasmere there are two trails: the Hound Trail, over ten miles and dating back to the first recorded Grasmere Sports in 1852, and the Puppy Trail, over five miles, which was introduced in 1930. They are run under the rules of the *Hound Trail Association,* and usually attract over twenty runners each. As well as providing thrills and a spectacle for onlookers at Grasmere, Hound Trails provide an absorbing interest for their owners and trainers, who can race their hounds two or three times a week — pads permitting — throughout the summer season, over the Lakeland fells and beyond. But, as with the Guides' Races and the Wrestling, a Grasmere victory has a lure of its own.

Each trail is laid at Grasmere, traditionally by two experienced trail-layers, who need to be of sound wind and limb, as well as familiar with the terrain. One man lays the first half of the trail, and the second starts at the half-way mark, or "split", and drags an aniseed rag along the ground, working his way back to the finish, thus completing the trail.

The same routes are taken each year for the Puppy Trail and for the Hound Trail respectively. The Puppy Trail on leaving the arena crosses the Ambleside to Keswick road. The puppies race South-Eastwards up Bracken Fell, then via the Yew Tree, across Dunnybeck Ghyll and on to Nab Scar. There is then a short steep climb after which the puppies swing left behind Alcock Tarn. After crossing Rowan Tree Ghyll they start to drop down the fell towards the bottom of Greenhead Ghyll.

They are now heading back towards the arena and after another steep climb emerge into view near Butter Crag, passing under Grey Crag, where the first flag for the Senior Guides' Race is placed. Finally a right-hand swing again brings them into view from the arena, on a straight downhill course to the finish.

The Hound Trail at Grasmere leaves the arena to the South-West. The first obstacles to be negotiated are the two stone walls on either side of the road leading into the village. Thence the route runs across fields in the direction of Silver Howe. The Grasmere to Langdale road is crossed after about three minutes' running, where hounds pass the old Grasmere sports field at Pavement End, last used in 1903. Hounds then run past Allan Bank, home of the poet William Wordsworth from 1809 until 1811.

They are now heading Northwards towards the Easedale valley and after another couple of minutes cross the Easedale road at Goody Bridge. They are still running across the fields to a point North of Under Helm farm where the road is crossed again, and they run the intakes at the foot of Helm Crag. After crossing Greenburn beck, hounds reach the intakes at the foot of Steel Fell. They now swing right-handed to the East, crossing the Ambleside to Keswick road just North of the old isolation hospital, on to the slopes of Seat Sandal. Hounds are now heading back towards the arena and come into view running the Dunmail Raise intakes. A circuit of Tongue Ghyll is then made before they are again in view on Stone Arthur. They run just above the bracken line and down into Greenhead Ghyll, where the Hound and Puppy Trails converge. And so they re-appear by Butter Crag and thence in full view down to the arena.

THE ASSEMBLY

As the appointed time for the Hound Trail approaches — and punctuality is the keynote of the Grasmere Sports — hounds and their handlers begin to assemble in the ring. As the baying of the hounds begins, so the general excitement mounts. The hounds are then lined up, held ready for release. But before the start is signalled, again traditionally, by The Rt. Hon. the Earl of Lonsdale, each hound receives a dab of identifying colouring on its head, in order to eliminate any possibility of sly substitution in mid-race! Then, amid a crescendo of yelping, the flag is lowered and the hounds are slipped. Off they rush,

THE START. *Hounds rush past the trailer, as he returns to the arena dragging the pungent trail-rag. Their first obstacles to negotiate are the two stone walls bordering the adjoining road, as they start on their ten mile trail.*

FIRST OBSTACLE. *Hound Trail at Grasmere 1974, the year of Shannon's farewell victory. Hounds leaping at the first of many fell walls as they leave the arena and set off for the ten mile trail.*

ANTICIPATION! *Half an hour later - binoculars at the ready as the leaders appear on the sky-line.*

REFRESHMENT! *End of the trail, to enticing feed-bowls.*

out of the arena, over fell walls and fields to the foot of Silver Howe to the West of Grasmere, and the rest of the sports are resumed.

THE FINISH

Some thirty minutes later the handlers re-enter the arena, bowl, whistle, leash and binoculars in hand, and line up along the far side of the finishing rope. All eyes are now focussed high towards the East. A buzz through the crowd, followed by shouts of encouragement, indicates that the leaders have been sighted, almost on the skyline. Soon they are traversing towards Butter Crag, down towards the tree-line, before turning back sharply, headlong down the steep slope to the finish. All this is viewed from the arena, with the fells acting like a stage back-drop, down which the hounds rush and finally emerge on stage, as it were, into the arena, to the traditional strains of "John Peel".

This is the point at which the handlers' whistles and voices are vital to the proceedings, because there is many a slip in the final stages of a Hound Trail, particularly at Grasmere, where distractions occur. Many a race has been lost because a hound has been distracted from the scent on approaching the sports field, either by the proximity of the spectators, or the temptation of a water trough. Others, when tantalisingly near the finish, slow to a trot, only to be overtaken by faster finishers. Hence the need for urgent encouragement from the handlers, as well as an enticement in the form of a small titbit in the feed-bowl.

A team of catchers is on hand, acting under the judge, to identify the leading hounds and place them in the correct order for their respective prizes, each catcher being responsible for a prearranged placing. When the placings have been sorted out, they are announced, usually as the last stragglers return.

For the owners, interest and reward extend well beyond the winner, because there are prizes for the first six, and also for the first and second "maiden".

BREEDING, REARING AND TRAINING

Methods of breeding, rearing and training hounds obviously vary with individual breeders and trainers. As in horse-racing, breeding is something of a gamble. Some of the great names have come from very modest parentage. These same hounds have frequently failed to produce offspring of high quality. But, nevertheless, it appears that there is always plenty of demand for a hound which has made its name trailing, once it retires.

Years ago the rearing of hounds used to take place on farms, but this is not so much the case today. Circumstances permitting, it would seem that it is better to rear and train a few puppies together, rather than singly, until the time comes to sort out the most likely trail hound on which to concentrate — the others being put up for sale.

Training methods differ, but the broad outline is as follows. The puppies are given the opportunity to learn to use their noses by running on the fells and moors, where they can put up some game. At about eight months they are introduced to the trail mixture on short trails. As progress is made the practice trails get longer, and fences and walls are included. Then comes the day when a trailer is introduced, running in towards the puppies, as in the trails that the puppies will eventually run.

Most trainers like to get their hounds used to company and the general bustle of the trailing scene. After a puppy has gained a bit of experience it will probably join in with a few others in practice trails. By the time the organised trailing season starts at the beginning of April, the puppy should be getting round the trail and, with luck, showing promise. But again, as in the case of two-year-old racehorses, it is not always the early developer that reaches the greatest heights in the end. Some fail to train on.

FAMOUS HOUNDS

The hounds, like their human counterparts in the Guides' Race, are of the lean and hungry type. But they vary considerably in size and colour. They also have their days, and their favourite trails — a fact that does not go unobserved by those who like to add a bet to the general excitement. It is interesting to note how the same names recur among the leaders at Grasmere, but naturally over a much shorter span of years than is the case with fell-racers.

In recent years the most famous hound at Grasmere must surely be Shannon, winner in the rain in 1970, in hot sunshine in 1971 and again on his farewell appearance, in his sixth season of running, in 1974. In two other years at Grasmere Shannon was

SHANNON, *trained to the minute, poses with his handler, Stanley Jackson from Borrowdale, before lining-up at the start of his farewell trail at Grasmere, in 1974, which resulted in his third victory. Always at his best over steep rugged fells, Shannon usually excelled at Grasmere. Owned by W. Jackson and trained by Victor Brownlee, of Borrowdale.*

HOUND TRAIL, 1971. *Ready for the start at Grasmere.*

GUIDES' RACE AT GRASMERE, 1971. *As the competitors line up for the start, the winner, Fred Reeves (number 5), is second from the left. The runner-up, Tom Sedgwick (2), is next to him.*

placed. His owner was W. Jackson of Borrowdale, where he was trained on the farm of Victor Brownlee, with assistance from Stanley Jackson with the exercising.

Shannon was born in April 1968, by Town Head Lad out of Busy Lass. His dam was aptly named, for she produced four litters, with a champion in each litter. Shannon soon showed promise, and was runner-up in the Puppy Championship, awarded on the season's results over all trails. He was at his peak in 1971 with thirty-eight wins, and in 1972 with forty-one — out of some sixty starts each year, which reflects his soundness and durability; the more so when one realises that it was on the high rugged fells that Shannon excelled.

After his triumphant finale at Grasmere in 1974, Shannon was retired, to the freedom of the farm and to a less regulated diet. He had already secured for himself a stake in the future, with seven litters sired by him and due to race the following year.

Other recent names of note at Grasmere include Torch Singer, winner of the Puppy Trail in 1971 and the Hound Trail in 1972; Denver, second in three successive years, 1971-73; Echo, winner in 1973 (and Champion Hound in 1974); and Rose and Crown, winner of the Puppy Trail in 1973 and a promising third to Shannon and Pisces in the Hound Trail in 1974.

Though these names, and others before them, cannot rank with human Giants of Grasmere, the Hound and Puppy Trails provide an unforgettable spectacle to regular visitors and new-comers alike. Long may they continue!

CUMBERLAND AND WESTMORLAND WRESTLING

Cumberland and Westmorland Wrestling

The wrestling at Grasmere is conducted under the rules of the Association governing the Cumberland and Westmorland style wrestling, founded in 1906. It remains to be seen whether the recent creation of Cumbria will alter the traditional name of this style of wrestling or the title of its governing body.

THE CONTEST

A more sporting trial of strength and reactions than Cumberland and Westmorland wrestling would be hard to imagine. Though the sport is not for the faint-hearted or weak-kneed, it does not involve trying to knock one's opponent sense-less. Nor does it bear the slightest resemblance to the theatricals that one can see on television. The very nature of the contest helps to make the decision clear-cut and final.

Chapter 4

Nor is the conclusion at all foregone in favour of the stronger or heavier man. In fact it is this element of uncertainty and surprise that makes this style of wrestling so intriguing, for contestants and spectators alike. As witness the roar that went up when Alan Davidson, a fourteen stone Northumbrian, whose previous Grasmere titles had been at the eleven, twelve and thirteen stone limits, felled the mighty reigning champion Wilf Brocklebank, a nineteen stone Lancastrian, in the 1973 all-weights final.

The two opponents, clad in traditional costume, shake hands and then manoeuvre for the obligatory hold, with hands clasped behind the other's back, with each man's left arm over his opponent's right. Once both opponents have their grip, the contest starts. Superior weight or speed may end a contest in seconds with an immediate throw. Or it may last for several minutes of evenly matched exertion, with swift feints and counter-feints and titanic heaves intermingled. Wrestlers have been known to be "blown out" (disqualified) for stalling or wrestling purely defensively, and the knowledge that this may happen normally ensures positive action.

STONE WALL BUILDER VERSUS SHEPHERD, *in the All Weights final in 1971. The winner, Wilf Brocklebank (left) shakes hands before wrestling with Peter Hunter, who tends a flock of Scottish Blackface sheep at Gilsland near the Border. Hunter is a familiar figure in Grasmere finals. He has five Grasmere titles to his credit - three at 12 stone and two at 13 stone. He has also appeared seven times as runner-up in All Weights finals - losing six of them to the Grasmere Champion with the most victories, Ted Dunglinson.*

TAKING HOLD. *This can be a lengthy process if both contestants are determined to obtain their favourite hold. Some prefer a high hold, others strive for a low hold. The bout can only start when "Both hold" is called. There can be no "snatching", with a sudden hold and an almost simultaneous jerk. Here two evenly matched champions, John Dennison and Tom Harrington, are getting to grips.*

The first to touch the ground with any part of his anatomy other than his feet, or to break his hold, is the loser. If both fall simultaneously, the umpires declare a "dog fall", and the wrestlers start again. Usually the victor gives the vanquished a hand up and the whole atmosphere is most sporting.

At Grasmere there are three umpires for each contest. The finals are decided by the best of three falls, and the earlier rounds by a single fall. Spectators at a modern Grasmere can expect to see well over a hundred contests decided, starting with boys and culminating in the day's climax — the All Weights final.

THE SEASONS

Unlike the other two sports described, wrestling also takes place in winter, indoors. Wrestling academies conduct regular training evenings throughout the winter, and it is here that the various moves are taught and practised, rejoicing in such names as the hype, hank, cross-buttock, outside stroke or inside click. Interest is maintained by internal competitions and matches against other academies. Academies are conducted at Kendal, Carlisle, Thropton, Garstang and Millom. These academies are the backbone of the sport, and provide an excellent social and sporting background for any young man with the enterprise to join, and the perseverance to continue.

The outdoor or grass season opens on Whit Monday at Pooley Bridge, on Lake Ullswater, and ends in early October at Wasdale Head. The World Cumberland and Westmorland championships are decided, at various weights, at various meetings throughout the North each year. But a Grasmere title remains a special achievement.

GIANTS OF THE PAST

GEORGE STEADMAN

The greatest name in the history of Grasmere wrestling was George Steadman, who achieved fourteen victories in the All-Weights wrestling at Grasmere, starting in 1872 and ending in 1900. During that long period other giants who challenged Steadman successfully for titles included Tom Powley (three times), George Lowden (seven times) and Hexham Clarke (three times). On Steadman's retirement, Hexham Clarke was Grasmere champion three years out of the next four, with the title going to George Steadman's son Maurice in 1903.

Steadman, who lived at Brough on the Pennines, was five feet eleven inches in height, and at the age of forty-six, and still winning, he weighed eighteen and a half stone. Steadman, despite his bulk, was reputed to be remarkably nimble on his feet.

TED DUNGLINSON

In 1948 there emerged a new Giant of Grasmere, Ted Dunglinson, an agricultural engineer who had first trained as a blacksmith. He was born at Brunstock, near Carlisle, and made his first appearance at Grasmere in 1947 at the age of nineteen, falling to a twelve stone wrestler, George Tweddle. But in 1948 he felled the 1946 All-Weights Champion, J. Carlile, a policeman from Kendal, in the final. Thus began an era of twenty years, during which Ted Dunglinson won fifteen Grasmere All-Weights titles, passing George Steadman's tally. Like Steadman, he was also busy elsewhere, winning over six hundred first prizes at wrestling. His peak year was 1954, when he achieved fifty-two victories, conceding only two falls. It is interesting to note that even he never went a whole season without a fall.

Ted Dunglinson wrestled usually at around fourteen and a half stone, and frequently had to throw heavier opponents, which makes his record all the more outstanding.

GIANTS OF TODAY

Dunglinson's supremacy was ended at last by a heavier, but not younger, man, who eventually got his measure—Wilf Brocklebank, a nineteen stone farm contractor from Tewitfield, near Carnforth. ended at last by a heavier, but not younger, man, who eventually got his measure — Wilf Brocklebank, a nineteen stone farm contractor from Tewitfield, near Carnforth.

WILF BROCKLEBANK

Brocklebank won his first Grasmere title in 1968 at the age of forty. In his younger days his wrestling activities were restricted when, as a farm worker in Scotland, leave off work was hard to obtain. But in his forties he has become the outstanding heavyweight wrestler.

But in this never completely predictable sport there is always the likelihood of a surprise, and this was provided in 1973 when Alan Davidson, who had previously won five Grasmere titles, at eleven, twelve and thirteen stone, and had now grown to fourteen stone, toppled Brocklebank in two straight falls. Davidson, who has a reputation for felling heavier men, had nevertheless fallen to Brocklebank twice in the previous week elsewhere. But with a Grasmere title in prospect, Davidson conjured up all his skill and timing, and gained the first fall. This he did by using his famous "hank" whereby a wrestler gets his legs twisted round his opponent's and by superior science in twisting and partly lifting at the correct moment, falls on top of his opponent. Davidson promptly repeated the tactic to gain the second fall. The history of Grasmere is full of such reversals. Another modern Giant, matching Brocklebank in solidity, and almost in size, is Joe Barnes, All Weights champion at Grasmere in 1969 and 1970.

LIGHTER CHAMPIONS

But not all the "Giants" of today are heavyweights. For instance a familiar figure is a shepherd from Gilsland, near Carlisle, Peter Hunter. He has won five Grasmere titles at twelve and thirteen stone, but it is perhaps as a runner-up in the All-Weights division that he is best known — six times to Ted Dunglinson and once to Wilf Brocklebank.

Further down the scale is Bill Bland, lightest of five wrestling brothers, sons of Gilpin Bland, who won six Grasmere titles between the wars. Bill managed to equal his father's tally when he won the eleven stone division in 1972.

Another busy wrestling family achieved a unique record in 1973, when Joe, Jim and Tom Harrington won three Grasmere titles in one afternoon, at eleven, twelve and thirteen stone respectively. Tom Harrington's skill and indifference to his opponent's weight has earned him Cumberland and Westmorland titles at these three weights concurrently. One of his sternest opponents is John Dennison, also a Grasmere champion of repute.

A glance at the records, as well as any present-day programme, will reveal that Cumberland and Westmorland wrestling tends to run in families. Besides the Blands and the Harringtons, there are the Davidsons, the Threlfalls and the Youngers well to the fore.

FAMILY RECORD. *For the first time in the history of Grasmere wrestling three brothers - the Harringtons - won titles on the same day. Champions, left to right, Joe (11 stone), Jim (12 stone) and Tom (13 stone).*

FATHERS AND SONS

Fathers often take their sons to winter academies or summer meetings. In 1973 both Boys' events at Grasmere, under fifteen and under eighteen, were won by boys whose fathers were also wrestling that day — David Stewardson and Wilf Brocklebank respectively. To the latter stands the unique record of winning the under fifteen and under eighteen Cumberland and Westmorland championships concurrently, as well as winning the latter three years in succession (1972-4).

It is certainly a sport at which father can vie with son, and brother with brother. In 1974 Wilf Brocklebank senior met his eldest son, Harry, in the All-Weights final. Harry, who was twice under eighteen champion at Grasmere was appearing, at the age of twenty-one, in his first Grasmere final as a senior. The receipt of twenty-five years was not yet enough to offset the concession of five stone and much experience to his father.

Much speculation arises as to which Brocklebank will take over the mantle of Wilf senior. But in any case it seems reasonable to prophesy that the name of Brocklebank, so prominent among the Giants of Today, will be equally so among the Giants of Tomorrow on Grasmere's historic sward.

GRASMERE'S WRESTLING CHAMPIONS

from 1852 to the present day

CUMBERLAND AND WESTMORLAND WRESTLING CHAMPIONS AT GRASMERE

	Heavyweight Wrestling	Lightweight Wrestling
1852	R. Bigland	J. Dixon
1865	J. Vickers	J. Coward
1866	J. Coward	J. Vickers
1868	D. Marr	J. Colleen
1869	J. Nelson	J. Allison
1870	M. Shearman	W. Litt
1871	H. Holmes	J. Graham
1872	G. Steadman	R. Powley
1873	J. Jones	J. Hodgson
1874	T. Powley	R. Powley
1875	T. Powley	R. Powley
1876	T. Powley	R. Powley
1877	G. Steadman	W. Matthews
1878	G. Steadman	W. Matthews
1879	G. Steadman	I. Frear
1880	G. Lowden	J. Moffatt
1881	G. Steadman	J. Moffatt
1882	G. Steadman	J. Moffatt
1883	G. Lowden	J. Simpson
1884	G. Lowden	T. Kennedy
1885	G. Lowden	J. Simpson
1886	G. Lowden	J. Robinson
1887	T. Kennedy	J. Bainbridge
1888	G. Steadman	J. Robinson
1889	G. Steadman	J. Robinson
1890	G. Steadman	T. Graham
1891	G. Lowden	J. Little
1892	G. Steadman	T. Graham
1893	G. Steadman	J. Little
1894	G. Lowden	W. R. Yates
1895	G. Steadman	T. Graham
1896	G. Steadman	W. R. Yates
1897	H. Clarke	W. R. Yates
1898	H. Clarke	J. H. Graham
1899	H. Clarke	W. R. Yates
1900	G. Steadman	W. Branthwaite
1901	H. Clarke	T. Graham
1902	H. Clarke	G. Jackson
1903	M. Steadman	H. Fisher
1904	H. Clarke	H. Fisher
1905	J. Bowman	J. Wallace
1906	J. Bowman	J. Wallace
1907	W. Studholme	W. N. Hutchinson
1908	W. Studholme	J. Wallace

In 1909 Middleweight Wrestling was introduced.

	Heavyweight	Middleweight	Lightweight
1909	W. Studholme	J. J. Ridley	J. Temple
1910	W. Studholme	R. Farrer	Finalists "blown out"
1911	W. Studholme	J. Little	J. Davis
1912	J. Robinson	A. Lowther	W. Jackson
1913	W. Ritchie	A. Lowther	T. Simpson

From 1914 to 1918 inclusive the Sports were abandoned.

1919	R. Graham	J. S. Robinson	A. Holliday
1920	Jerry Jackson	J. Jackson	W. Robinson
1921	J. Adams	F. Preston	H. Kitchen
1922	D. Clark	W. Robinson	W. Jackson
1923	W. Knowles	G. Bland	J. S. Noble
1924	D. Clark	G. Bland	H. Kitchen
1925	W. Knowles	J. E. Johnston	W. W. Logan
1926	W. Knowles	J. E. Johnston	E. Keith
1927	D. Clark	J. A. Johnson	R. Greatorex
1928	D. Clark	R. Hayhurst	J. B. Winter
1929	J. Jackson	J. F. Robinson	T. Blakeney
1930	W. Knowles	S. Knowles	J. Grisedale
1931	J. T. Brewer	S. Knowles	H. White
1932	J. T. Brewer	T. Hayhurst	H. White
1933	G. Brewer	G. Bland	F. Blakeney
1934	D. Clark	G. Bland	H. White
1935	J. T. Brewer	G. Bland	H. White
1936	J. T. Brewer	A. Bracken	W. Hall
1937	J. T. Brewer	A. Wannop	J. Carruthers
1938	J. Spedding	G. Bland	F. Blakeney
1939	F. Wilson	J. Dixon	F. Blakeney

From 1940 to 1945 the Sports were abandoned, during the Second World War.

1946	J. S. Carlile	A. Wannop	M. Sewell
1947	J. T. Brewer	T. Pritt	J. Carr
1948	J. E. Dunglinson	T. Hayhurst	R. S. Steele
1949	B. Huddlestone	R. Carter	H. Coulthard
1950	W. Bragg	R. Mason	G. Wilson
1951	J. E. Dunglinson	T. Nicholson	J. Telford
1952	T. Little	R. Mason	H. Coulthard
1953	J. E. Dunglinson	C. Bragg	J. T. Richardson
1954	J. E. Dunglinson	G. Wilson	J. T. Richardson

In 1955 the weights were altered.

	All Weights	**12 Stone**
1955	W. Knowles	J. Bland
1956	J. E. Dunglinson	P. Hunter
1957	J. E. Dunglinson	P. Hunter
1958	J. E. Dunglinson	P. Hunter
1959	J. E. Dunglinson	J. J. Bland
1960	J. E. Dunglinson	C. Bragg
1961	T. Mason	J. J. Bland
1962	J. E. Dunglinson	J. J. Bland
1963	J. E. Dunglinson	T. Mason
1964	J. E. Dunglinson	R. Robson
1965	J. E. Dunglinson	A. Davidson
1966	J. E. Dunglinson	J. J. Bland
1967	J. E. Dunglinson	J. J. Bland
1968	W. Brocklebank	J. Bland
	11 Stone	**10 Stone**
1955	F. Coulthard	J. T. Richardson
1956	T. Bland	J. T. Richardson
1957	J. Bland	G. Wilson
1958	A. Coulthard	G. Wilson
1959	P. Hayhurst	G. Wilson
1960	W. Bland	G. Wilson
1961	P. J. Hayhurst	J. T. Richardson
1962	J. Bland	G. Wilson
1963	B. Armstrong	J. T. Richardson
1964	B. Armstrong	G. Wilson
1965	W. Bland	J. T. Richardson
1966	G. Wilson	(No Lightweight)
1967	A. Davidson	W. Bland
1968	A. Davidson	W. Bland

In 1969 the weights were again altered.

	All Weights	**13 Stone**
1969	J. Barnes	A. Davidson
1970	J. Barnes	P. Hunter
1971	W. Brocklebank	A. Davidson
1972	W. Brocklebank	P. Hunter
1973	A. Davidson	T. Harrington
1974	W. Brocklebank	P. Hayhurst
	12 Stone	**11 Stone**
1969	C. Bland	J. Dennison
1970	R. Robson	W. Bland
1971	T. Harrington	J. Dennison
1972	E. Younger	W. Bland
1973	Jim Harrington	Joe Harrington
1974	T. Harrington	I. Armstrong

SPECTACULAR FALL *to G. W. Younger in the 1973 11 stone final. But Joe Harrington won the Championship by the odd fall.*

ACTION PICTURES

The pictures which follow record some of the
spectacular contests of recent years
in the historic Grasmere arena

Who's Fall?

13 STONE FINAL 1974. *Peter Hayhurst, a farmer, gains the deciding fall over Wilf Brocklebank junior, the Boys' under eighteen champion. A seemingly convincing fall for Hayhurst, but on a strict interpretation of the rules, and with the aid of the camera's speed, could it be argued that Hayhurst has broken his hold before Brocklebank has touched the ground or released his hold? Wreslters instinctively tend to release rather than fall right down on an opponent, in order to minimise the risk of injury to either contestant.*

Both hold

Going!

Going!

Gone!

ALL WEIGHTS FINAL 1972. *Wilf Brocklebank, the reigning champion v. Donald Dayson. Brocklebank won by the odd fall.*

WORLD CHAMPION *at three weights (11, 12 and 13 stone) Tom Harrington gains the winning fall over another Grasmere and World Champion, John Dennison, in the 13 stone final, 1973, thereby reversing the decision when they met earlier in the afternoon in the 11 stone wrestling. The speed, skill and timing of both these wrestlers enables them to compete successfully in higher weight divisions.*

LANDING WITH A THUD. *John Dennison defeats Harry Brockle-bank in the 13 stone semi-final, 1973, under the watchful eye of one of the umpires, J.S. Noble, light-weight champion at Grasmere in 1923.*

BATTLE OF THE GIANTS. *Wilf Brocklebank (Grasmere Champion in 1968, 1971 and 1972) meets Joe Barnes of Renwick, (Champion in 1969 and 1970) in an evenly matched semi-final in 1974. Barnes, eighteen stone and notoriously hard to shift, succumbed to the strength and skill of Brocklebank, nineteen stone, after some mighty heaves.*

HISTORIC MOMENT AT GRASMERE. *W. Bland, from a famous wrestling family, equals the record of his father Gilpin Bland, with his sixth victory, over S. Dalton, in the 11 stone final in 1972.*

BROTHERLY ENCOUNTER. *Harry Brocklebank hoists his younger brother, Wilf, before depositing him on the turf. Both have won numerous Boys' championships, and are sons of the Grasmere and World Champion, Wilf Brocklebank senior. Harry made history at Grasmere in 1974 by reaching the final against his father. This was the first father versus son final at Grasmere. The father won in straight falls on this occasion, but there could well be some more family finals in future years.*

MOMENT OF SENSATION. *Alan Davidson (14 stone) about to fell the reigning champion, Wilf Brocklebank (19 stone) at Grasmere in the 1973 All Weights final. Davidson's right leg is poised for the quick use of the "hank", round one's opponent's leg, which he brought off twice to win by two clear falls. One of the delights of Cumberland and Westmorland wrestling is the ever-present chance that with skilful timing, a giant may be toppled. Davidson, from Northumberland, had five previous Grasmere championships to his credit at lighter weights, but this was his first All Weights victory.*

SHEPHERD VERSUS SCHOOLMASTER. *Peter Hunter (left) and Roger Robson take their holds in the 13 stone final, 1972.*

HUNTER'S FALL. *He defeated Robson, a former 12 stone Grasmere champion by two falls. This was a skilful contest between two of Grasmere's finest wrestlers.*

THE WRESTLING RULES

The rules followed in
Cumberland and Westmorland style wrestling

The Wrestling Rules

The official rules followed in Cumberland and Westmorland Style Wrestling are shown below:

WRESTLING RULES

Published by the Association Governing the Cumberland and Westmorland style of Wrestling. It is laid down:

1. That all competitions be open for FREE COMPETITION TO THE WORLD (in the Cumberland and Westmorland Style) except where otherwise specified.

2. That an allowance of 2 lb. only shall be made to any wrestler beyond the weight specified; that no one shall be allowed to weigh in in any other costume than that in which he intends to wrestle; and that no wrestler be allowed to wrestle except in becoming costume; and that any wrestler once weighed in is weighed in for the whole competition, unless the referee orders him again on the scale. The weighing machine shall be placed near the edge of the wrestling ring, and all wrestlers shall be weighed in in full view of the public as far as is possible.

Chapter 5

3. That all competitors shall pay an entrance fee of not more than
    10p and any wrestler attempting sham wrestling, personation, buying
    or selling a fall, getting into any weight to which he is not entitled,
    or otherwise misconducting himself, or in any way attempting a
    "barney", tending to bring discredit on fair and manly wrestling,
    shall upon detection be at once expelled, and at the discretion of
    the Governing Board debarred from again contending at any sports
    meeting affiliated to or registered with this Association and his
    name shall be forwarded to all Sports Bodies who are members of,
    and affiliated with, this Association.

4. That no competitor be allowed more than one entry in any one
    competition; and that at the end of every round a fresh draw shall
    be made, and that no further entries be taken in any competition
    after the draw for the first round has begun.

5. That the name of every wrestler shall be called three times, and
    anyone not answering the third time shall be "blown out". All
    competitors shall enter in their own names, but an assumed name
    may be adopted by a competitor, provided that he has the name
    registered with the Secretary of this Associaton.

6. That every fall in every competition shall be judged by two judges,
    and a referee, who shall be appealed to only if the judges disagree.
    The decision of the referee shall be final, and, further, he shall be
    empowered to decide any point not provided for in these Rules.

7.   That three minutes be allowed in which to take hold, and in the event of the hold not being obtained, the judges shall allow the wrestlers an additional two minutes, and the wrestler then refusing to take hold shall immediately be disqualified.

8.   That Competitors shall shake hands on entering and leaving the ring, but no talking whatever shall be allowed. Any competitor breaking this rule renders himself liable to be immediately expelled.

9.   That when both men have got hold and are fairly on their guard, play commences on the word of the referee, and, with the exception of kicking, the wrestlers are allowed to use every legitimate means to throw each other. To strike with the side of the foot shall not be deemed kicking.

10. That if either party breaks his hold, that is looses his grip, though not on the ground, and the other still retains his hold, the one so leaving loose shall be the loser. That in the case of slipholds occurring in any bout, the referee has the power to stop the bout and tell the offender to correct this hold, and warn him as to his future conduct. The referee may suspend one or both wrestlers from further participation in the contest.

11. That if either man touch the ground with one knee only, or any other part of his body, though he may still retain his hold, he shall not be allowed to recover himself, but shall be deemed the loser.

12. That, if both fall to the ground, the man who is first down, or falls under the other, shall be the loser; but if they fall side by side, or otherwise, so that the umpires cannot decide which was first on the ground, it shall be wrestled again.

13. That if it comes to the knowledge of this Association, either at the time of the contest, or afterwards, that any "barneying" or unfair arrangement has taken place, it must inquire into the matter, and deal with the parties concerned in such a manner as the Governing Board may determine. Any wrestler, observed, or known, to buy, sell, or to compromise a fall, or disobeying the umpires, will be refused payment of any portion of the prize to which he otherwise may become entitled. No wrestler shall be allowed to "lie down" to another under any circumstances without the consent of the referee. That in cases where the judges and referee are unanimously of the opinion that a wrestle is a "barney", they shall have power to suspend the wrestlers, the matter to be reported to the Secretary of this Association within three days of the day of the said offence, and the Governing Board of this Association shall fix the term of suspension of the offenders.

14. That no competitor shall be odd man more than once in any competition.

15. That where there are twelve entries and under, in championships only, the best of three be wrestled all through the competition.

16.   That wrestlers who still "follow the ring" will not, under any circumstances, be permitted to officiate as umpires, or referees, and any wrestlers known to officiate in these capacities render themselves liable to suspension at the discretion of the Governing Board.

17.   That all objections to wrestlers after the first round on account of over-weights, or otherwise, must be referred to the referee, whose decision shall be final.

18.   That the Secretary of this Association shall supply copies of the Constitution, Bye-laws, and Wrestling and Academy Rules at 10p each and shall impress upon competitors and all Sports Bodies the necessity for having and studying them.

BRIEF GLOSSARY OF WRESTLING TERMS

Glossary of Wrestling Terms

BRIEF GLOSSARY
OF WRESTLING TERMS

*The Kendal Wrestling Academy Instruction Book.
Cumberland and Westmorland "Chips".*

HYPE

Lift your opponent; then strike inside or outside his knee. Inside for "inside hype" and outside for "outside hype". Strike with either right or left leg. Right is much more popular especially for "inside hype". Good left leg hypers are seldom seen nowadays.

SWINGING HYPE

Same as above, but swing at the same time as lifting.

BUTTOCK

Get your buttock under your opponent's stomach as a
fulcrum and throw him bodily over. A slack hold is best,
just below the neck most effective, and half the game in
buttocking.

CROSS BUTTOCK

Same as above, only cross your leg (left usually) over your
opponent's left leg above the knee and bring him forward
over your left leg. Right leg buttock — exactly opposite
way round for right leg buttock or cross buttock.

HANK

Getting your leg twisted round your opponent's so that he
cannot free it. Then by superior science in twisting and
partly lifting at the correct time force yourself over him
when he must fall over.

BACK HEEL

Put your heel against your opponent's heel, pulling his leg
towards you and push hard with your chest at the same
time, thus forcing him over backwards.

OUTSIDE STROKE

Strike opponent's right leg with your left, just above the ankle, forcing opponent to your left — no lifting necessary — opposite way round for right leg outside stroke.

INSIDE CLICK

Clicking inside your opponent's heel and forcing him back, can be done both left and right. Always slacken hold after clicking inside your opponent's heel. This is most effectively done by a swing off the chest and apply when opponent touches the ground.

CROSS CLICK

Click opponent's heel with your left heel. Pull his leg towards you at the same time, throw your chest forward — a case of pull and push — the quicker the better as in all chips.

HOLD

When taking hold keep left elbow down and force right hand over as far as possible; always keep your chest as low as possible. Attack is the best defence.

COMPETITORS IN 1974*

Event 6. HEAVYWEIGHT WRESTLING (All weights)

Competitors must book in by 2-30 p.m.

Prizes:—Each man falling in Third Round, £1; Fourth, £2.

Each man falling in the Semi-Final to receive £5.
FINALS: First, £30 and the **"Kennedy Cup"** to be held for one year; Second, £15; Third £5.

Name	*Address*	*Name*	*Address*
H. Armstrong, Carlisle		J. Harrington, Calthwaite	
I. Armstrong, Carlisle		Jos. Harrington, Calthwaite	
J. Barnes, Renwick		T. Harrington, Carlisle	
S. Bell, Stirling		W. Harrison, Silloth	
C. Bland, Arnside		P. Hayhurst, Hale	
J. Bland, Arnside		S. Hull, St. Michael's	
J. J. Bland, Levens		P. Hunter, Gilsland	
W. Bland, Kirkby Malham		T. Mason, Crosthwaite	
R. E. Blenkharn, Ings		R. McGregor, Longtown	
J. A. M. Bracken, Catterall		A. Millington, Millom	
H. Brocklebank, Tewitfield		B. Molloy, Thistleton	
W. Brocklebank, Snr., Tewitfield		J. Pringle, Rothbury	
W. Brocklebank, Jnr., Tewitfield		R. Robson, Carlisle	
S. Dalton, Coanwood		A. Southward, St. Michael's	
A. Davidson, Thorneyhaugh		R. S. Steele, Brunstock	
G. E. Davidson, Warkworth		C. Stewardson, Meathop	
G. M. Davidson, Warkworth		E. Threlfall, St. Michael's	
K. Davidson, Rothbury		H. Threlfall, St. Michael's	
J. E. Dunglinson, Brunstock		W. C. Threlfall, Woodplumpton	
J. G. Elliott, Langholm		E. Younger, Thropton	
A. Harrington, Kirkbride		G. Younger, Thropton	
G. E. Harrington, Kirkbride			

1st.. 2nd.. 3rd..

MEMBERS AND OFFICIALS

MEMBERS AND OFFICIALS
OF THE
GRASMERE SPORTS COMMITTEE

THE GRASMERE SPORTS COMMITTEE LIMITED

Members and officials at the time of the 1974 Sports.

PRESIDENTS

The Lord Lieutenant of Cumbria

The Lieutenant of Cumbria

The High Sheriff of Cumbria

The Earl of Lonsdale

Sir Fergus Graham

The Earl of Carlisle

V. S. Howard, Esq., Chairman, N.W. National Trust

P. J. Liddell, Esq., Chairman, N.W. Water

LIFE MEMBERS

Mrs. & Mrs. T. S. Austin
R. Barratt, Esq.
Mr. & Mrs. C. Baxter
C. J. D. Borwick, Esq.
Mrs. & Mrs. A. B. Brown
J. B. Carruthers, Esq.
Mr. & Mrs. C. H. Cheetham
Miss E. J. Cheetham
Major M. J. Clarkson-Webb
Mr. & Mrs. John Coney
R. S. Crosfield, Esq.
E. R. W. Dent, Esq.
Mrs. B. A. P. Dobson
Mrs. B. G. P. Dobson
C. H. J. Dodd, Esq.
E. C. Dodd, Esq.
J. H. Dodd, Esq.
J. R. Q. Dodd, Esq.
M. W. L. Dodd, Esq.
G. D. McD. Dodd, Esq.
J. B. Dykes, Esq.
Sir John & Lady Fisher
Mr. & Mrs. J. A. Fell
J. R. A. Fell, Esq.
J. H. Fell, Esq.
R. A. Fell, Esq.
Mrs. M. Fitch
Mr. & Mrs. R. Fothergill
Capt. R. L. S. Gaisford
C. D'O. Gowan, Esq.
Lt.-Col. T. R. L. Greenhalgh
R. G. Grice, Esq.
A. G. F. Hall-Davis, Esq.
Mr. & Mrs. Hart Jackson & Family
Major T. W. I. Hedley
Major J. W. B. Hext
Miss S. Hey
Mrs. O. Y. Hibbert
Lt.-Col. J. D. Hibbert
L. Hodgson, Esq.
H. Hornyold-Strickland, Esq.
Lt.-Cdr. & Mrs. T.
    Hornyold-Strickland
H. C. Hornyold-Strickland, Esq.
W. N. L. Howard, Esq.
J. F. O. Huthwaite, Esq.
M. W. Huthwaite, Esq.

G. J. K. Harrison, Esq.
Wing-Cdr. E. A. Keegan
Mr. & Mrs. M. H. R. Kennedy
M. H. B. R. Kennedy, Esq.
J. F. Lafone, Esq.
Brig. R. G. Lewthwaite
The Countess of Lonsdale
Mrs. P. Lowry
G. V. Martin, Esq.
N. Marquis, Esq.
D. A. Marquis, Esq.
A. J. S. Marsh, Esq.
H. Middleton, Esq.
R. Nelson, Esq.
W. Paton, Esq.
P. F. Rabbidge, Esq.
Miss H. Read
Mrs. N. Rigg
Major & Mrs. M. E. M. Sandys
M. R. K. Sandys, Esq.
Dorothy, Lady Scott
F. C. Scott, Esq.
Mr. & Mrs. P. F. Scott
Sir O. & Lady Scott
Misses C. & M. Scott
E. Shaw, Esq.
Mr. & Mrs. M. C. Stanley
O. H. Stanley, Esq.
N. Stanley, Esq.
Mrs. D. R. Stokes
R. Stokes, Esq.
Mrs. A. Thomas
B. L. Thompson, Esq.
Mrs. N. Troughton
Brig. C. E. Tryon-Wilson
W. Twentyman, Esq.
R. Wace, Esq.
G. C. W. Waite, Esq.
Lord Wakefield
Mrs. J. Webster
F. Welsh, Esq.
D. H. While, Esq.
H. V. Wilkinson, Esq.
J. C. Wilson, Esq.
Mr. & Mrs. J. W. Wilson
Miss A. Woodburne
J. R. C. Woodburne, Esq.

COMMITTEE

F. B. Hart Jackson, Esq.
(Chairman)
J. H. Harris, Esq., J.P.
(Vice-Chairman)
Brig. C. E. Tryon-Wilson,
C.B.E., D.S.O.
Capt. R. L. S. Gaisford,
O.B.E., R.N.
M. C. Stanley, Esq., M.B.E., D.L.

O. R. Bagot, Esq., T.D., D.L., J.P.
J. A. Cropper, Esq.
Major J. Ulf Machell, M.F.H.
Major C. H. Cheetham
Rt. Hon. the Earl of Lonsdale
A. C. Cavell, Esq.
J. B. Dykes, Esq., M.C.
Lt.-Col. R. Barratt, M.B.E.

SECRETARY

G. A. Ashton, F.C.C.A., F.C.I.S., Rydal Road, Ambleside

FOOTRACING OFFICIALS

Handicapper: T. C. Young

Starter: W. Tallantire

Timekeeper: J. J. Payne

Bellman: W. Kirkby

TRACK OFFICIALS

Referee: P. L. Davidson

Judges: T. Newby, J. Richardson, H. Martin, R. Spiers

Marksmen: R. Hutton, W. Rickerby, J. Johnston, J. Wise,
F. Winder, W. Airey, W. Dixon

Field Telephone: J. Heath

Lap Counter: J. Craig

Prize Cards: C. Weir

L.S.P.A. Secretary: S. Gibson

WRESTLING OFFICIALS

Umpires: J. J. Ridley, S. R. Knowles, J. W. Handley,
A. E. Dennison, W. Hudspith

Wrestling Manager: W. W. Edgar

Referee: J. S. Noble

HOUND TRAIL MANAGER

K. Bunting